You are a STAR little one...
SHINE BRIGHT!

Written by
Sylva Nnaekpe

Copyright © 2020 Sylva Nnaekpe.

All rights reserved. No part of this book may be reproduced by any means, medium, graphic, electronic or mechanical, including photocoping, recording, taping or by any information storage retrival system without the written permission of the author except in the case of brief quotations embodied in critical articles and reviews.

Books may be ordered through bookstores or
by contacting Silsnorra Publishing at:
silsnorra@gmail.com

Due to the dynamic nature of the internet, any web address or links contained in this book may have changed since publication and may no longer be valid. The views expressed in this work are solely those of the author and do not necessarily reflect the views of the publisher, and the publisher hereby disclaims any responsibility for them.

ISBN: 978-1-951792-96-1 (Soft Cover)
ISBN: 978-1-951792-97-8 (Hard Cover)
ISBN: 978 1 951792-98-5 (Electronic book)

Printing information available on the last page.

Silsnorra Publishing Review Date: 03/04/2019

Change starts with you, and there are great resources around you that will help you succeed. Use them.

First, you must believe in yourself,
and you will achieve so much.

Air is life. Take the time to breathe.

It will help your body work properly.

Take the time to be quiet.

It will help you think and act better.

Take the time to listen.
It will help you understand and communicate better.
Take the time to reflect. It will help you gain a better understanding.

Take the time to explore.

It will help you learn new things.

Take the time to love, care, and respect one another.

It will help you become a great leader and a good role model.

Learning is fun.

Take the time to learn.

It will help you grow and improve yourself and your community.

Learning is fun.

Take the time to learn.

It will help you grow and improve yourself and your community.

Take the time to read something new every day. It will keep your brain active, healthy, and up-to-date.
Take the time to ask questions. It will help you discover new things to help yourself and others.

Take the time to dream. It will help you to achieve any goal you want to achieve. Take the time to build. Hard work always pays off.

Take the time to win.

It leaves you with a satisfying and refreshing feeling.

Discover your gifts. Take advantage of them and learn to master the things you love and believe in.

Do not let anyone or anything deem your shine or tell you - you can't achieve success in the things you believe in.

REMEMBER,

change starts with you,

little one. Believe in yourself,

and you will achieve so much.

You are a STAR little one...
SHINE BRIGHT!

THE END

Follow@ ivrydbook

to see more.

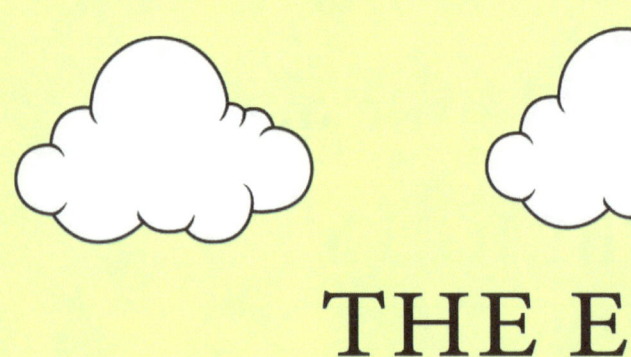

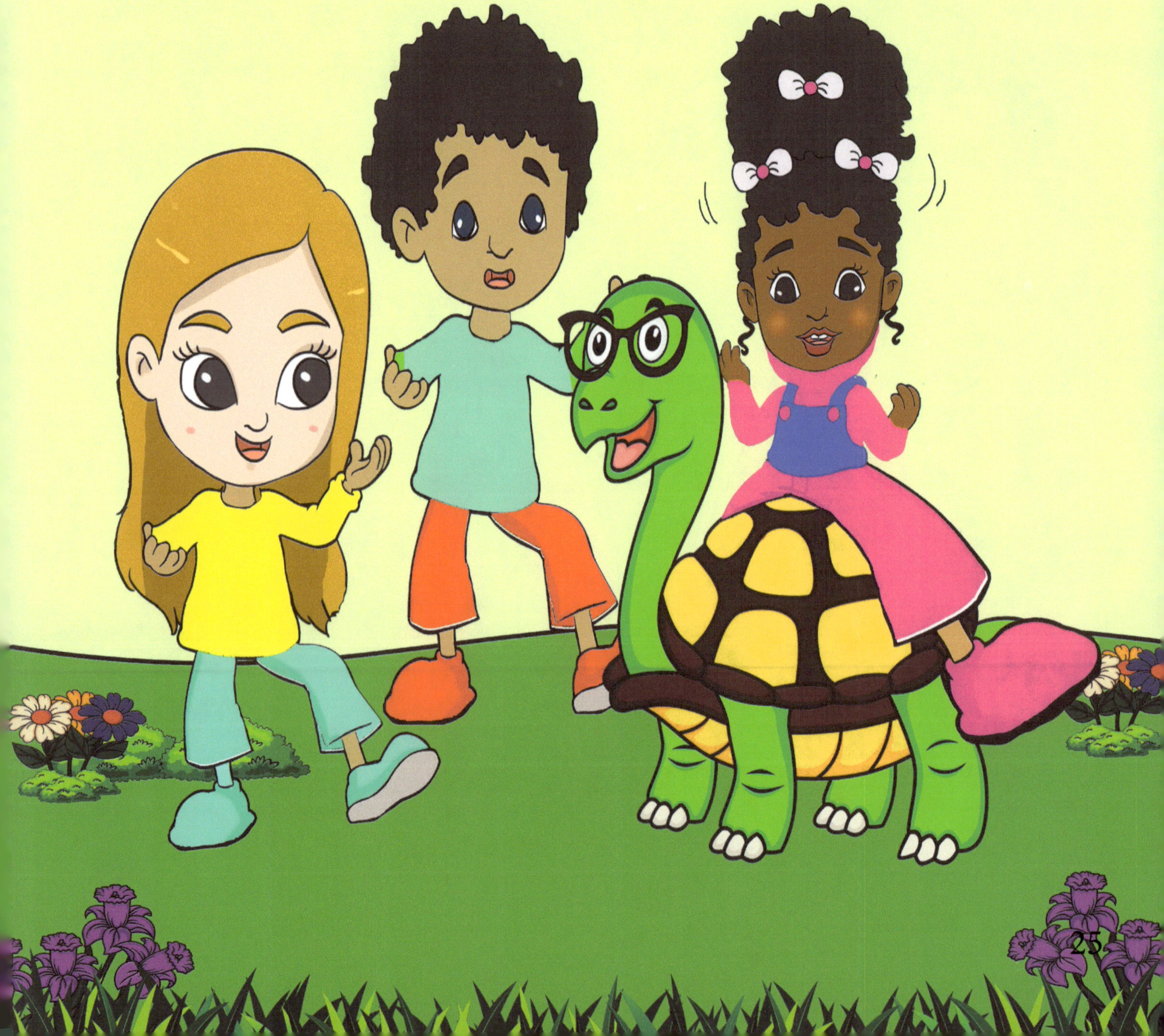

www.ingramcontent.com/pod-product-compliance
Lightning Source LLC
Chambersburg PA
CBHW050752110526
44592CB00002B/46